DISCLAIMER

The contents of this book are not based on therapeutic evidence. It is not intended to be used in place of any recommended practice. It is the author's account of her own healing, which at various times has been facilitated by professionals and medication. Healing is an individualized process.

The author's process began and continued as it did because she had no insurance benefits from 2008 until 2011 and every attempt at sliding-scale therapy fell through. She believes that those things happened for a reason and chose to research what accepted therapies were being used and do what she could do on her own. A little over a year into her recovery, she chose to visit her family doctor, a trusted friend and Christian physician. Together, after a lengthy disclosure, they made a decision as to what medication would further facilitate the author's progress. This decision was not an easy one to make; however, his simple explanation made complete sense. "If you were in need of thyroid medication, would you deny yourself that cure?" The medication that was decided upon has worked and has not changed the author's personality or caused any other issues to date. The author and family physician continue to monitor her health to ensure that this course is necessary and continuing smoothly.

Another professional who was also included along the way was a person who had been working in substance abuse recovery for over 30 years. A random connection was made when the author began a new work project and a close working relationship revealed his experience. A friendship developed that allowed the author to trust the individual enough to let him assist her with some cognitive redevelopment. While he is not a therapist, his vast experience and knowledge in the field of addictive behaviors proved helpful, as sexual abuse leads to similar thought addictive thought processes.

The most important thing for the reader to remember is that healing cannot take place in isolation, as the author's friend Angela Williams of Voice Today, Inc. is often heard stating. Whether you are just beginning your journey into healing or have been walking it for decades, you need a team of people who you can trust to love you at all times.

Please see the appendix for additional resources.

God's Promise of Victory

Iris Subel Davis

Energion Publications
Gonzalez, Florida
2012

Cover Picture: Iris Subel Davis
Cover Design: Henry Neufeld

ISBN10: 1-938434-08-0
ISBN13: 978-1-938434-08-2
Library of Congress Control Number: 2012946221

Energion Publications
P. O. Box 841
Gonzalez, FL 32560

energionpubs.com

850-525-3916

TABLE OF CONTENTS

FOREWORD

Life as I had always known it ended on September 21, 2006, at 4:30 a.m. The death that morning of the man I had loved, lived with, married, had a child with, took care of, fought with, and loved some more ended a chapter in my life. What was in store has been one of the most beautiful love stories that I could ever have hoped to be a part of, truly. My prayer is that every reader will connect themselves somewhere in this story and that God will begin the process of writing their own personal love story with Him.

May His words come through more than my own. As Paul said in 1 Corinthians 2:6-10.

We, of course, have plenty of wisdom to pass on to you once you get your feet on firm spiritual ground, but it's not popular wisdom, the fashionable wisdom of high-priced experts that will be out-of-date in a year or so. God's wisdom is something mysterious that goes deep into the interior of his purposes. You don't find it lying around on the surface. It's not the latest message, but more like the oldest—what God determined as the way to bring out his best in us, long before we ever arrived on the scene. The experts of our day haven't a clue about what this eternal plan is. If they had, they wouldn't have killed the Master of the God-designed life on a cross. That's why we have this Scripture text:

No one's ever seen or heard anything like this,
Never so much as imagined anything quite like it
What God has arranged for those who love him.

But you've seen and heard it because God by his Spirit has brought it all out into the open before you.

CHAPTER 1

Death can bring about so many things. For me, it brought about a personal healing. That healing began when, after the death of my husband Victor in Atlanta, I realized that I wasn't grieving the way I thought I should be. The grieving process is different for everyone, but the key word there is process. It seemed to me as if I had not even begun the process. I knew there was something wrong the moment I realized it; but, like everything during grief, it was just a fuzzy thought. I managed to slip it into the mental trunk of "I'll deal with this later" and continued walking the steps that I had to at that time.

Those steps included a grief class, where I learned how to grieve, literally. But, the "feelings" just were not there. I wanted them to be, so badly. I just couldn't understand why they weren't. Experiencing the death of someone so close for the first time had thrown me into a whirlwind of emotions, triggering what most professionals might call a post-traumatic stress disorder episode. Hindsight is the only reason that that statement can be made. While going through it, I literally thought I was losing my mind. It wasn't the first time those words had taken a hold of me. I reacted the same way when I lost my virginity at 16, when I found out I was pregnant at 24, when I had cancer at 34, and to varying degrees at other pivotal points at my life. What was wrong with me?

Three months after Victor's death, my house was emptied, with all my belongings packed and ready to be shipped to Florida. Through a dream, the Holy Spirit had spoken to me that I needed to go home to Florida. Me being the petulant child I had always been thought that meant NOW. My daughter, Lindsey, and I lived in an empty house on air mattresses for 6 months before that vision became a reality! During this time, I continued to struggle with getting on with life and beating myself up over not truly grieving for the loss of Victor. Something was just not right; but as I often did, I blamed myself for not being "like everyone else" and not being able to truly feel connected to the loss of someone who was so important in my life. I sought solace in reading the Bible, reading mountains of Christian books, listening to countless hours of wonderful Christian music. There was no doubt for me that the Lord Himself was with me during that time; the only doubt I had was in myself. I literally believe now that I was running away from a pain that was most likely the worst pain that I had experienced in my conscious life. I simply did not have the skills to deal with it. Buy why not?

The question stayed with me over the next two years as I returned to my hometown, Pensacola, FL, to start life over. Or, as I thought at the time, to continue a life that had been interrupted by our move to Georgia. While I was there, remnants of a life long ago buried began to emerge. It had been over fifteen years since I had had any desire to be with any man other than Victor. For me, due to unknown issues, being married is what saved me from myself. During our marriage, I followed all the rules of being married because that is what I knew to do. I never suspected that hidden within there was a reason that I didn't WANT to follow the rules. I just assumed that I was a "bad" person like I had been all of my life and buried the thoughts I had of other men during my marriage. I struggled during this time with seeing my marriage for all that it was—the good, the bad, and the ugly, literally. There were parts of me that began to surface that not only was I ashamed of but literally afraid of coming to light again being back in Pensacola.

One Saturday, I felt the Lord leading me to take a drive. I ended up visiting many places in town that had significant meaning to me in my past life. Most of them, oddly enough, had to do with places that were connected to promiscuous behaviors from teenage years and my very early childhood—as far back as first grade and wanting to kiss a certain boy at a birthday party. During that drive, I clearly recalled the day I accepted the Lord as my Savior. I was barely 4 years old, and scared to death that I was on my way to hell. Not just worried, but knowing that I was headed there. That memory shook me to my core—what is in the mind of a 4 year old that gave me the knowledge that I was so bad? Being a teacher, I have seen many kids who, at that age, are oblivious to anything other than home and school. Sadly, that wasn't the case for me. On that drive, I was reminded of all that was in my mind from a very early age—boys and sex. But, the reminder was not condemning or convicting in nature; it was as if I were being shown something that I needed to know. I just didn't know what yet.

One particular night in 2008, after I had been seeing an old boyfriend in Pensacola for a few weeks, I made a desperate phone call to a very dear friend. I called her from the back porch of little church and proceeded to tell her that I had no clue why I was wanting to proceed in this relationship when I knew it was toxic. It was bringing up old tendencies of promiscuity and other behaviors that I had long since put down. Why, after so many years of walking so closely with God, was I having these thoughts and desires? My friend, a recovering addict, gently told me that I sounded like an addict. The concept was nothing new to me. I had lived with an addict for 18 years and knew full well what the throes of the cycle of addiction looked, felt, and sounded like. I had just never seen my own behavior because it was always overshadowed by that of my husband who was an alcoholic and recovering drug addict. You see, that's what I saw addiction as—the substance, not the deeper cause. I connected it to such because it was the substance that was the problem in my warped mind. I could never see that there was a root issue causing an addict's behavior. That is, until I became the addict.

In that moment, I realized that I was, and had always been, addicted to sex, or relationships at the very least. I still wasn't ready to deal with all that that implied, but I accepted that I was an addict that night. I remember looking at the revelation that I was an addict more intently than anything else. Suddenly, many pieces of my life fell immediately into place. This incident coupled with the drive that the Lord had take me on were fitting together somehow. Though the thoughts were fuzzy, my life as I had known it was beginning to make sense. Freedom as I had never known it started coming at that moment. If no other point comes through clearly in this book, please know this: God is a gentleman. He never forces anything on you. He allowed me to come into full understanding of what was in my life in my own time and at my own pace, and He never left my side.

The very next day, I received an email from a friend's prayer chain in Atlanta to pray for a woman who had been sitting at church the same night that I was on the back porch learning that I was an addict. While on her back pew, a man walked into the back of the church and proceeded to expose himself to her which caused her to have a flashback. The man was immediately apprehended, removed, and arrested. The woman was taken immediately into an office where she was ministered to while the memory of a childhood event continued to emerge that night. She received counseling, prayer, and began the process of living with the knowledge that something bad had happened to her so many years ago. I replied to my friend, Wow. If I could receive my deliverance like that, I would take it. On the back porch, I had told the Lord in desperation, I don't know why I have this or what it is, I just don't want to feel like there is anything between us anymore. I asked Him that night to deliver me. I asked him to forgive me for not being able to understand what Victor had gone through and to have mercy on me even though I had not had mercy on Victor at times.

The day after the email came, I called another friend and traveled to Atlanta to receive prayer. It was during that prayer time that the Lord ministered to me and gave me the name of a man whom I had not thought of in over 25 years. I was stunned. I knew who he was and that he had died when I was 12 years old. I drove home to Pensacola, deep in thought and experiencing another new level of freedom.

Things really began falling into place that night. Every question mark that I had in my mind about parts of my life came into clear focus. I had always wondered why I had some of the problems I had with boys, drinking, and dabbling in drugs. My life looked like a good life: great parents, nice house, good school—but I myself didn't feel or think like I came from a "good" home. I never understood that, and my mother even made comments throughout my life that she never understood why I had such low self-esteem. She was right, and that was another issue that I used to beat myself up about.

During that drive, I also realized that certain behaviors I had as a child were not rooted in a desire to be a bad person. I was simply doing what abused children do: act out what has been done to them. The memories of those incidents along with concrete memories of how I played with all of my dolls confirmed to me that I had indeed been abused. As a teacher, if I had seen a child doing all that I had done, I would know that they had been or were being abused. I finally began accepting that about myself.

Upon arriving home, over the next few days, I explored my past memories through intense journaling sessions. I recalled clearly a period of my life where I had been deeply afraid—something that is out of character for me. I remember having intense leg cramps during those times and that my mother would stay up with me at night, rocking me and singing to me. I also noticed, through photographs, that my physical features changed drastically over a 6 month period of time. I went from looking like a precious little baby to an almost grown adult in my face. I'm not sure how some readers will take this next statement, but it must be said. Sin was introduced into my life at the point of my abuse—and everything, even my physical features, began to change at that moment. I was 3 years old. The point that I accepted Christ was during my kindergarten year, where I entered when I was 4 years old. During that same year, while my parents were away at my mother's 20th high school reunion, I accepted my first communion—a very clear and precious memory to me. I believe He allowed me to have those memories so that I would understand at this time in my life that He had always had His hand on me, even though it might seem otherwise. Without that timely understanding of His constant presence in my life through that one clear memory, I might have suffered a more debilitating emotional breakdown as I began to deal with the reality of what had happened to me as a child.

Months later, as I was continuing to deal with this, a woman whom I had never met before or have seen since, came to me at a church service and prayed with me. Hardly any words were spoken; I just fell into her arms and started crying. She told me afterwards that the Lord had told her that I had been violated when I was a little girl. That night, acceptance ended and the work of healing REALLY began.

While the revelation that something bad had happened to me was in some ways devastating, it was also a point where I understood that God's love had saved me all of my life. There had been many close calls as I lived my life, but I never went over the proverbial edge. Maybe He didn't allow that because I was always asking Him, why am I like this—I don't know the answer to that. I do know that He created our minds and my mind protected me from the knowledge that I had been abused until I was spiritually, physically, mentally, and emotionally ready to deal with that knowledge.

CHAPTER 2

Once the past was brought into the light, things did not just immediately begin to change for the better. Now would be a good time to talk about the fact that while my journey was beginning, there were a few people who did not want me to walk down this path. I love everyone of them for trying to protect me. I understand, in hindsight, that they had no idea what they were saying to me. We have since talked about this issue, and they apologized for their lack of understanding of what I was experiencing at that time. Because of who God is in all of us, we forgave each other and grew closer from the whole experience. They have continued to encourage me as no others have by standing by me through every second of my walk, even when we may disagree as to how I walk it at times. My journey would not be complete without each and everyone of them, and I hope they know that. I have tried to let them know that as often as possible. I learned from the good and the bad, and I feel confident that they would want me to share this part of the journey as others may go through this as well. Their responses were probably not that unusual and that is why I feel the need to tell the reader to be prepared for such a reaction. Beyond doing what I sensed the Lord leading me to do, I had to do what I believed was right for me, regardless of what others thought.

Sexual abuse is not a comfortable topic. It is uncomfortable for the victim, the families involved, friends, co-workers, and I would guess the perpetrator. When I decided to deal with my issues, it meant that those closest to me were going to have to deal with them as well, or we would not being seeing or talking to each other while I was dealing with them.

Sadly, that was true in some cases. I learned who could handle my issues, who could not, how much they could handle, and when to let it just be between me and God. I learned to have compassion for those who were seemingly holding me back.

Being the way I am, I tried to analyze why they wanted me to stop. I realized that my pain was a reminder to some of them of their own pain. My dealing with mine was dredging up things for them as well—not always about the same issue. Pain is a reminder of pain period. I had to learn that they were not rejecting me even though it felt that way. I was often left alone to deal with things. They were turning away from the pain, not me. Going through this process was almost as painful as dealing with the abuse itself. But, I am thankful for it, because it matured me. And, boy, did I need that!

Most people have their the emotional growth stunted after abuse occurs. I had indeed always felt younger than I was. I even questioned this about myself over the years. I was mature in most ways, but so immature in others. It was very confusing for years. During the first year or so of recovery, I almost suffered a mid-life crisis. Somewhere along the way, I realized that I was over 40 overnight. I remember the realization of living almost a half-century hitting me one day. Not living in the present moment had literally caused me to lose a couple of decades. One day, that loss was mourned for several hours.

Not living in the moment is a normal reaction to what I lived through as a child. In order to escape the pain of abuse, the victim displaces themselves in any number of ways. Imagine doing this for decades and then all of a sudden realizing that it is not normal to do such a thing. When I "woke up" to this fact, I was older than I was in my displacement. I began to want to live in the moment after I realized how much of my life I had been living in the future and in the past—anywhere to get away from the present pain that I was suffering. The abuse had ended so many years before, but the inability to deal with any pain was something that was with me everyday until the revelation came about. The desire to change was there, but the road to change was just beginning.

Another stumbling block at the beginning of the journey were some ministry-types who told me "It's all under the blood, just get on with your life. You're doing this to yourself by looking back. Stop being so negative." I think these responses upset me the most. I have never understood people who were like this. It is directly un-scriptural. I hope my editor doesn't change that word! I do not mean that I do not believe that it was all under the blood of Jesus—I knew beyond knowing that it was. But speaking those words did not change me, as much as I believed them and wanted it to be so. I still had real and natural issues that had to be dealt with. My mind still reacted normally to the act of sexual abuse. This reaction triggered a learned response to trauma that was repeated throughout my life until I recalled the abuse.

David bared his heart and soul throughout the Old Testament, and I never heard the Lord tell him he was less of a person for digging through his issues. In fact, it is the baring of his inner soul to God Almighty that brought them closer together. Not only did David speak to God about His power, but he spoke to God about his own misgivings and insecurities as a man. It took consequences and tests from God to work out of David his issues, even after David confessed them with his mouth. The verbal confession was only part of the process. When a minister cannot handle that full process, well, I'm sorry—I just have to wonder to the Lord, is this someone who can speak into my life? There is no judgment in that statement. The only thing in that statement is a desire to be discerning of who to trust to come into the inner circle of my life. I had to learn that that inner circle was not big enough for everyone and to only allow those who understood that total process into my daily life and circle of mentors.

I never believed that the Lord allowed me to begin the journey to stop it. He had never done anything else in my life that way, so why would this be any different? If He was taking me there, He had a purpose. Who was I to question that? Trust me, I did—many times. Those were the times that I chose to stop the journey. I mean, sometimes, it was just too heavy to deal with. That is the truth. But you know, when I was rested and ready to move forward in my "life"—I always came back to the same place in my daily walk. The Lord GENTLY led me through the steps that I needed to walk. My strongest hearts' desire was to be in His complete and perfect will—I told Him over and over, "I do not want to settle in life this time around." That means getting rid of what He tells me is not Him, not just what I choose to get rid of. And, I have to trust Him in that process, even now. This was and is all about Him, first and foremost.

Once I realized that the Lord did indeed want me to deal with this life-changing revelation, I had to accept that He was about to change my life. Change MY life? Why? I could quote enough scripture to answer that question for years, but my insides did not match the words that I knew by heart.

Abused children are taught not to think very highly of themselves. All through school, I remember looking at other children everyday wishing I could be like everyone else. Back then, I did not understand why I felt so different. I felt guilty for wanting to be like them. I was smart enough to know that I had a good life, but I felt so different. Because I was so young when the abuse occurred, I did not have the memory of the actual act to filter into my understanding of why I felt the way I did. It stayed, as traumatic memories often do, shrouded in a safe place until the person can emotionally handle the entire memory.

When I realized that my actions and thought patterns had been unknowingly influenced all of my life by such a horrible act, I was almost devastated. I remember feeling as if my entire life had just ended. It had, in a way. It was the destruction of the old Iris that made a way for God to rebuild me into who I already wanted to be—a new creature in Him.

Letting go of that old Iris was the hardest thing I ever did, up until that point. I do not mean habits like drinking, drugging, or promiscuity—those were gone on the outside just because I knew they were wrong. By the old Iris, I mean my thinking patterns, responses, and reactions that were the clues to the past—all of those had been built upon the lie that had entered my life the moment the man violated me. At that moment, I began to believe that I was worthless, unwanted, unloved, ugly, disgusting, hardened, undesirable, a throw away. I continued to believe that even after my mid-twenties where I had enough sense to understand the meaning of the Word of God. But, it was as if the words could not make it down where I needed them the most.

I began living the words out of my mouth but suffered through years of hiding what was really going on inside. It seemed like everyone else was getting it, but not me. I could not feel what I wanted to believe so much. The night I was on the back porch, it felt like I had been transported back in time to 15 years earlier when I began to walk with Christ in earnest.

I told a close group of friends who ministered to me countless times over the next two years and still do at various times now. We are much more than friends; we are family. I began to become a regular at the local bookstore's abuse section. I read what seemed like hundreds of articles and books about sexual abuse victims, their perpetrators, family dynamics, repressed memories, survival techniques, therapy suggestions, and success stories. I also read about how abuse affects individuals in their marriages and their sex lives. I learned why I had responded to my husband in certain ways. Sometimes, it was like reading stories written about my own

life. I will never forget how much self-acceptance I gained
through that time period.

Once I realized that I was different from everyone else
for a reason, I stopped thinking that there was something
wrong with me for thinking that I was different in the first
place. Read that sentence again. That knowledge allowed me
to begin to deal with what I needed to change in me that was
based on erroneous perceptions from the abuse. I began to
replace all those old patterns with new information, and this
time, they stuck with me like glue. Why? Because the lie that
was hidden in me that was twisting everything was exposed
and had been rooted out.

During this time, I had two friends who I chose to reveal
all the details about the abuse to. One was a man, and one
was a woman. Neither was extremely spiritual, but both are
Christians. They had had difficult lives at various times and
were no strangers to the ugliness of life. They were friends
who had been with me through difficulties that needed explaining, and together we all received closure on some of
those difficulties as they helped me through this time of
emptying. I spent countless hours on the phone with both
of them, crying, ranting, raving, cursing, hating, and finally
letting go of the most devastating incident in my life. Not one
time did they flinch about anything I told them, no matter
how graphic or disrespectful I became during those conver-
sations. They loved me unconditionally and supported me
without judgment as I emptied myself completely. They did
not ever, much to my chagrin at times, offer one word of advice, one word of correction, or one word of admonition for
what I was saying. I write all that not to demean any of my
other friends, but to help the reader understand that a person may be needed who can handle the nitty-gritty details
of the story should discussion be needed. That need became
evident for me when I began to need to express shock over
what had happened. I needed to not be alone during this

step; and God made sure that I was not. Once the ugly is out and exposed in the light, it will not come up again the same way. Its impact is limited after a full disclosure.

Maybe because the abuse happened at such an early age, I never had the words to tell anyone. I mean, think about it. How does a three year old explain something like that? I was telling people by my actions, but a lot of those were done in secret. No one could hear me. On this journey, there was a time when I found my voice. As an adult, I knew what needed to be said, and I needed to say it for myself. All of my friends consoled me and affirmed me in my shock, something I needed to hear as an adult. One important thing here, they never let me stay there too long.

Probably the most important thing I did during those many months was to journal extensively. Memories began to come out; feelings were fully explored; hang-ups were discovered and worked out; and general freedom started to flourish. Journaling frees a mind of worry and anxiety. It removes the fears and concerns from your brain activity and demobilizes them, for the most part. It is still something that is a part of my life, and probably always will be. Most of these journals are put up now; but every now and then, I will take a couple of them out and read through them. Not to remember the past, but to see how far the Lord has brought me. I thank Him for all the painful times that are recorded there and are now gone from my mind. I also thank Him for all the good times that are recorded as well.

In those entries, it became clear to me that I was not who I always thought I was. I was more. Before the reveal, I could not see that very well. As the layers of the old Iris came off, I could see a little girl hidden inside that was still holding onto her dreams of long ago. I had a talk with her one day. I told her that she had done an incredibly brave thing, protecting me all these years. I told her that she was strong to have held onto our dreams for us. I asked her to trust me to take hold of them now, and I told her she could have fun living life now. (See Appendix A.)

After setting her free, I began to see things about myself that I had never realized about myself before. It was hard to accept that the Lord had a plan for me that did not include dysfunction. But, He does! It involved me learning who I was before I could begin to live it, though. I took several personality profiles and spiritual giftings test. The reason I did this was because I learned that the true person that God designed me to be had been buried under the baggage that came along with the abuse. I had to thoughtfully think about myself as I had never done before. It was uncomfortable at first because I was still learning to love myself.

So many people struggle with allowing God to love them because they do not love themselves. I believed that I had to perform in order for God, or anyone else, to love me. The abuse taught me that, and I never had anything to correct that perception. The sad part is that an abused child seeks to be loved with every performance, always to be let down.

God loves us unconditionally—a concept that is in direct conflict with what an abused child is taught. A child who has never been abused receives that information without an opposite concept to cause a miscompute. An abused child cannot understand unconditional because conditions are engrained on their mind first. The younger the abuse, the deeper engrained the idea that love looks like all give and nothing in return. That becomes a learned attitude. Even as an adult, a survivor has these thoughts—and that's why abuse needs to be dealt with. It needs to be understood that the thing causing the disconnect which is the abuse is a lie.

Revealing it and dealing with it can take away the disconnect. With it gone, a person can begin to truly receive love the way it was intended to be received. After all, isn't being able to receive and give love is a fundamental principle to living a full life?

CHAPTER 3

Diving into a process as deep as healing from sexual abuse can seem more than a little scary—no matter if you are at the beginning, middle, or "end." I do not believe that the process really ends; I believe life just gets easier to live.

Abuse of any kind conditions a person to live in a heightened mental, emotional, and mental state. There are many physiological and mental effects that become "normal" for individuals. Speaking from my own experience, I was inundated with physical ailments such as colds, allergies, skin problems, recurrent infections, and a general sense of feeling sick most of the time. Nothing I ever did, no medicine I ever took, ever made me feel better. My immune system was comprised, and compounded by internal and external stress, I was physically sick.

My emotional health was also affected. My tendency was to blow everything out of proportion. When I say everything, I truly mean everything. The smallest incident involving my husband, my children, bills, work, or friends became a dramatic event. Those types of mental and verbal reactions had not only a mental effect but a physical one as well by keeping my adrenaline pumping almost continually. I know I was an adrenaline junkie. I think that was the first thing I realized, at least a decade before I was able to deal with the abuse. Living a chaotic life was not fun, and I constantly sought ways to make my life better. Without the key piece of information as to why I was living that way to begin with, though, they were all futile.

There are several key points in my life that occurred where I seriously questioned my emotional stability. They all happened prior to the reveal of sexual abuse. I am going to list them without discussing them because it is their collective importance that is the focus.

The first was when I lost my virginity at the age of 16. The second was a major marital crisis. The third was after I received a cancer diagnosis in 2000. My reactions were, respectively, running away from home for 2 weeks, trying to commit suicide, and a complete breakdown. A fourth could be the death of my husband (my first close loss), after which all of this came out because I chose not to respond in any of those ways due to my more mature emotional age—even though it was still lacking to some degree.

When viewed in isolation, a pattern is visible. Traumatic events brought about dramatic response. True to my self-destructive tendencies, I berated myself for having the responses instead of understanding that there was a reason I responded the way I did. Others in my life who I compared myself to responded in a far more reasonable manner to the same situations. The reason I responded the way I did was an earlier, traumatic incident that brought about my responses when similar emotions surfaced during subsequent events. I was living with Post Traumatic Stress Disorder (PTSD) and did not have a clue.

The term PTSD was familiar to me only in terms of soldiers coming home from war. Since I had never been in the military, did not have inexplicable nightmares, or walk around trying to kill another person, I never dreamed that I had such a disorder. After the cancer diagnosis in 2000, I entered into a short series of classes on mind, body, and emotional health and their connections to help me deal with such an obvious trauma. In addition to those classes, my oncology group had a therapist on staff. My doctor recommended that I see her. I worked with her for a period of 3 months, during which time she diagnosed me with "Adjustment Disorder." That was only scratching the surface, however. Upon reading the definition, causes/incidence/risk factors, and symptoms, I was grateful to have an understanding of what was happening to me in that moment. However, in hindsight, I see that no one (not even myself) was asking why I had "adjustment disorder." It was no one's fault; and credit for timing certainly belongs to God on that. It was this one isolated diagnosis that actually helped me accept the truth of PTSD almost 10 years later.

There are countless articles, interviews, and books about PTSD. I have read a lot of them, before and after my reveal. I thought I understood what it was all about until I had an episode AFTER I knew what it was. It was pretty scary. And there have been more than one. I will give an example in the next paragraph, but I'd like to say first that part of the healing from this portion of sexual abuse involves the victim understanding that what is happening to them is only a response to a similar emotion. The response is not an indicator of anything other than that something happened in the past. It is in no way a statement about who the victim is now or ever was. The emotions that come up during an episode are real and cannot be ignored. In my opinion, placations or proverbial advice only exasperates what a victim is feeling.

It is important for anyone witnessing such an episode to understand that the person in a flashback is experiencing reality—the reality that something in their present is reminding them of their past. That reality is that something in their past was beyond their control and that they have emotions that need to be dealt with. Victims need understanding, empathy, and a calm guide to remind them that they are in the present and that what they are feeling is a momentary response to something that is going to pass. The middle of a flashback is not the time to try to "speak sense" into someone. That information will be lost in the throes of a flashback, trust me on this. I desired nothing more than validation, assurance, and comfort during my many episodes—and that hasn't changed. What has changed is the way I handle myself.

It is like learning to ride a bike. The training wheels eventually come off; you might still wreck every now and then; but for the most part, riding the bike of life will be a joy.

Not long after my reveal, I went to work for a friend's organization. Due to the type of organization it was and the history of those working there, we were very open at times about our life issues and prayed for each other often. One time, a co-worker and my supervisor came to me in an accusatory manner. They were together in an office, talking to me by telephone on a speaker phone. Neither of them would allow me to speak or to present my side of what had happened. Even though I was in my own home, completely secure, I started having a panic attack. The situation doesn't matter, only that I had done nothing wrong and in the end, my supervisor saw that and my co-worker was spoken to, as was I, regarding certain things. I say that to illustrate the emotions that were coursing through my body and mind as I was having to deal with this situation. I was still in a hyper-awareness state as I was learning to understand my reactions and responses in terms of all this new information. Experiencing the emotions of not being able to stand up for myself in a seemingly benign situation brought on a physical response to what was being triggered in my mind and emotions.

This was not the first time I had experienced something like this. It was just the first time that I knew why I was reacting the way that I was. Immediately, it seemed as if I were watching myself in a movie. I was able to observe myself, every reaction, every thought, and every response in a way that I had never done before.

That situation contained every emotion that an abused child feels: isolation, intimidation, manipulation, suppression, helplessness, fear, anxiety, shock, anger, betrayal, and distrust. Looking back, I remember how violently those emotions were coming at me during that incident. The situation itself became blurry to me as all I could focus on were the larger-than-life emotions and my reactions to them.

I remember trying to cry but not allowing myself to do so and immense hatred toward both parties (one acting as the perpetrator and one acting as the parent in the work situation). I completely shut-down on that phone call. I believe with all of my heart that my supervisor, who had known me for quite some time and was aware of the abuse, recognized my out-of-the-ordinary, over-bearing silence as an indicator that something else was going on other than what we were discussing. The Holy Spirit completely intervened in that conversation and touched his heart to change his handling of me. He, being who he is in his heart, stopped his tirade against me and began to listen to not only my explanation but my unspoken pain. At the moment that I knew I was about to have an emotional break-down due to the triggers, God intervened and helped me realize in a nano-second what was really going on. I followed His and my supervisor's lead and was able to maintain semi-composure. Only after the completed phone call did I collapse into a heap into the Lord's arms. He was the only one there. I remember feeling like a child who had faced up to the school bully and won and went around the corner to throw-up.

No one could tell me that that would happen or that in that moment that what I was really feeling was a response to the molestation itself. The two of them were not thinking about that, and I wasn't either. That is, until I began to feel the feelings. Since then, similar incidents have come up. Thankfully, those responses have improved as I am able to judge better what is at work within me. Only now, three years into recovery, am I able to employ some of those at times pert, little platitudes such as "Let Go and Let God." I love all of them, and they are very true. It's just that it has taken a long time for them to come up first in my mind instead of the pain and anxiety that can still surface during a trigger situation.

After the reveal, the trigger incidents were always involv-ing a negative aspect of the abuse. However, I am finding that this is not always the case. Another example will follow this explanation. You see, there is another aspect of healing that should be discussed. It was touched on in an earlier chapter. It is the subject of what can feel like flippant comments to "change your attitude" and "stop being a victim." Those are two important steps in healing, yes. However, as an adult who had repressed the memory of what was actually causing attitude issues and victim-mentality, I would like to say that even on my best day I could never overcome what was in my hidden heart—no matter how many times I recited any scripture or phrase. And, I always put myself down for not being able to do that, even without knowing why I couldn't do it. I didn't even understand what I was trying to overcome because I had nothing in front me to fight. What I felt I was fighting was who I was, at that time—and how do you fight yourself? I never did; I just hated myself more.

After the reveal, I was able to completely understand why I had always felt so badly about myself. It was clear to me why I felt different; I was different in that something had happened to me. However, I was not different than anyone else who has issues in their life. That newly, leveled playing field motivated me to strive for what I had always wanted in my deepest heart of hearts—a normal, full, and happy life. I began to speak against all the negative things in my mind after I learned what they were. All the positive tools that I had collected in my life were finally able to work. I had finally gotten to the root of why I needed them.

With all of that, I could get on with living life, right? Well, yes; and I have. But this is the part that needs to be heard in context of those last two paragraphs. While "living life" there are positive aspects of living that I am having to learn to live with because I have never lived them without those trained, emotional negative responses. My brain doesn't know what it doesn't know. I only know now what I am NOT supposed to do. I'm having to learn what TO do. Forty years of habits don't change overnight, but they do change.

This situation happened just recently involving a positive aspect of the healing and was regarding being able to trust. After experiencing a less-intense response during a recent situation with a girlfriend, I recognized that something was wrong. I pulled up some information regarding PTSD and indeed discovered that I was still responding to something even though I didn't know what. After reflecting over the situation, I realized that I was upset because it felt as if my friend did not trust me to do something that I do. My initial response was to back completely out of the proposed agreement that we were working on. However, after I researched my perplexing physical and mental reaction, I concluded that my friend had no idea of how she was making me feel—she was just asking me a question. I knew that if I walked away in my current mindset that the agreement would not be the only causality. Our friendship was liable to be sacrificed. My solution was to pray and counsel because I was in new territory. I wanted to run but not at the expense of losing something important. After hearing an objective view on my responses, I approached my friend in an honest and open fashion. I told her that several of her questions made me feel as if I were not being trusted of being capable and asked her to forgive my edginess toward her. She in turn apologized for making me feel that way without knowing it. I had to self-explore, re- evaluate with that knowledge, take a risk of exposing my feelings, and then risk relying on what I thought our friendship was made of— it worked out. We were solid, and we're both better for that experience.

You see, I don't think like this all the time. I did at first. It took almost a year for me to stop analyzing every situation in terms of the abuse. Thankfully, I had gotten laid-off from my full-time job at that time and was living on unemployment. I consider that year God's gift to me to be able to learn about myself in a safe environment with limited situations that moved along at a manageable pace. I was a real mess for quite awhile. Quite the way I know children are immediately after their abuse. I was just an old child.

Another massive part of my healing was dealing with being alone. Since I don't have all the pieces of what happened to me, I'm going to say that I must have wondered where my help was when I was being molested. I have no memory of not being without someone in my life: family, friends, men. I never allowed being alone to be an option for me. I couldn't. I did not know that I was even afraid to be alone. I just prided myself on the fact that I always had someone—especially men.

After my husband died in 2006, I really had no desire to be with anyone like I had in the past. At least not using my actions as an indicator. It was in my mind that I ran away to the solace of being with someone. That was another early indicator that something was wrong. Through circumstances after my husband's death, I moved from Atlanta, GA, back to Pensacola, FL, where most of my healing took place. I began living alone in Florida in 2009. I was about 15 miles from family and friends which was too far out for anyone to come and see me on a regular basis. That distance grew to over 350 miles in less than six months as the Lord moved back to Atlanta that same year. I have been in Atlanta, living alone, since 2009—something that I would never have been able to do prior to learning about the abuse. The abuse created the façade of my being alone with no one to care for me when I needed it the most.

Through one person's selfish act, abandonment became a part of my emotional make-up where it had never been before. Nothing could make up for that because I was too young to understand that those moments were just moments. I had no affirmation that everything would be ok because I did not have a voice, words, or concept of what had/was happening to me. The fear of being alone and rejected was born and took root as nothing else has during my lifetime.

The fear of being alone clouded all of my judgment, all of my life. What semblance of boundaries or good judgment I might have had just from common sense and getting older was completely obscured by not being able to handle not being with another human being. I forgave every person's every fault, tried to "fix" them, and compromised every fiber of who I was to forego being alone. That opened the door for many other issues to come into my life such as promiscuity, drinking, drugs, pornography, and many other ills that wreaked havoc on me as a person as well as my life. The very things that I grasped to fill in the blanks actually created more of the same. I remember feeling completely defeated one time after a weekend of partying. It wasn't just an issue of doing things I knew to be wrong in the sight of man and God, it was knowing that what I was reaching for wasn't working and what I was going to need to do next to feel better. Would the next thing be the one thing that made me forget how bad I felt forever? Would the next man be the one man who would never leave? Honestly, the merry-go-round may have stopped years ago; but, the music had kept playing inside of my head for years. One day, through this process, I realized that I could be a different person if I would allow God to heal me of being alone. And He has.

The only relationship that I have ever had that has ever filled every gap, fulfilled my every desire for true intimacy, and bolstered me to live what I believe is with Jesus Christ, the Son of God. Only He can do that. It is through the dynamics of my relationship with Him that I am learning how to truly love others for the first time in my life. It sounds so cliché, right? I used to cringe when I heard people say that. But, reader, you must understand that there is not one person on this planet who will ever accept you exactly the way you are right now and love you into who He made you to be.

Abuse told me that I was someone that I was not. It made me believe things about myself that God never intended me to believe. It made me feel that I was not worthy of anything in my life, whether I worked for it or not. It told me that people gave to me to get something from me. It changed who I perceived myself to be; but, it did not change who God created me to be. It does not change what I am called to do in this life. It does not have the power to destroy me—unless I let it.

Chapter 4

The Present is not somewhere that I ever enjoyed being. Like most kids, I'm sure, I dreamed of getting older to be able to do things reserved for older people—getting married, working, driving, drinking, having children, living on my own. Just the normal things that teenagers think about, I guess. The only issue is that these things were not passing thoughts for me. I planned and plotted, to some degree, how I would accomplish all of these things long before I was ever even a teenager. At the very least, I immersed myself in fantasies of what my life would be like with these things in them. Every opportunity was a magic carpet ride to another world. Every relationship became the vehicle to get me to these delusional destinations.

Looking back at my young life, or what I can remember of it, I see how much of my time was rooted in this behavior. It took me away from so much. The saddest part is that by the time I figured out what I was doing, I had been doing it for as long as I could remember. The act of disassociation had become one of my greatest talents; and, let me just say—I was very good at it.

For me, disassociation must have begun the moment the man hurt me. You see, in the moment that the act occurred, the worst damage was not the physical abuse. That is unconscionable, yes. But, worse still is the picture of innocence being ripped apart. A child, safe in his own thoughts and appropriate understanding of the world, is violently brought into an emotional place that he has no understanding of to any degree. His present becomes full of unbearable physical pain, immense fear and panic, and an overwhelming awareness of betrayal and abandonment. He is dangling above a moment in time, unable to comprehend what is happening. An escape mentality is born. From that point, whenever those emotions or any other unpleasant sensations arise, the behavior of mental escape continues.

During the last three years, breaking the habit of disassociation has been one of the most difficult challenges. Going to fantasy keeps a person from feeling certain pain, yes; but, it also keeps a person from dealing with and living in the present moment—which is where the joy of living truly is. By disassociating, I pushed aside the pain and/or joy that was right in front of me. The harm in doing that is that by not allowing myself to experience pain, I was denying myself the opportunity to learn how to lessen my future pain. I was denying myself a growth opportunity that would serve me in my future. Feeling pain is not pleasant, but the pain only lasts as long as it lasts. At the age of 3, pain is never-ending. Fearful of living in pain for what seemed an eternity, my mind shut down to the present and took me somewhere else that it deemed safe. As a 3 year old, I had no choice but to go there. A psychological norm saved me from a life that could have been filled with so much worse than it was, but the norm became a trap for me as I grew.

When I was older, the disassociation did not stop. Rescue fantasies were a favorite of mine. Now, I know why. In my little child's heart, she desperately wanted and needed someone to rescue her from that moment of violation. I realize now that, for most of my life, I was living a different life in my head and trying to make my real life look like that unrealistic picture. The pain of not achieving that unrealistic picture slowly became greater than whatever present pain that I was trying to escape. I could see that happening through the years, but I was helpless to stop it without the piece of why I was doing it in the first place. It was a habit that I did not recognize as a habit—I thought everyone thought that way and was just better at navigating life than I seemed to be. It is hard not to be ashamed of what I put my family through all those years, holding them to perfection that would never exist. We have worked through most of that and are stronger for it, thankfully.

The hardest part was putting down the habit of fantasizing and not picking it back up. That required me to deal with all the emotions in every situation that came up after I learned about the abuse. Learning to do that was an enormous change in my life—one that I did not think I would ever be able to do with ease. It has taken a long time, but it is finally becoming an action that I no longer have to stop and think about. A new, positive habit is being born.

I am now in a place where when a situation arises, most of the time, I pray through it fully aware of the why's and how's of what I am feeling. There have been some times where the ground was so new that I felt as if I were sinking in that new ground. I still pray; but, sometimes, I need another voice to help me because I do not know what I do not know. That is when I call upon that trusted group of friends who I know love me no matter what. I know that I know that they pray for me and are trusting God for my complete healing— just like me. God has used our mutual love for Him and each other to restore what was taken away from me at such an early age. It is that knowledge that gives me confidence to come to them when I need to. If for some reason they are not available, I do not take it personally anymore. I recognize that they, too, have lives and that whatever I am going through is not life or death like it used to feel.

That self-absorption mentality is typical for abuse survivors. Being self-absorbed is a learned behavior as a result of feeling abandoned and/or rejected. As an adult, I am consciously aware that I was not really abandoned or rejected by anyone. I was severely wounded by a person whose one horrific act made me feel abandoned and rejected. There is a difference.

There are many things in my present over the last 3 years that have been unpleasant. Learning to deal with those has been a challenge. I have learned through those challenges to let go of the "why is this happening to me" mentality. I no longer see every event as a punishment like I did in the past. When things do not go the way that I want them to, I have learned that there is a valid reason why they have not happened the way I would like them to happen. The main reason, I have learned, is that when you live your life for the Lord, He is in charge of your life—if you are truly living by faith.

For years, I lived my life the way I wanted to and when it became a mess, I would ask Him to fix my mess. Only recently have I learned to live each day in that day, making decisions based on sound judgment and trusting the Lord to work things out without my interference. Living in the present, for me, has come to be about what is His purpose for me THIS day. It means finding joy in the moments of THIS day. And there have been so many since my healing began.

One of those day-by-day, present moments involved the forgiveness of the man responsible for the things I lived through. Even while writing that sentence, I am aware of the fact that even he is not responsible. Sexual abuse is not an isolated incident. The perpetrator is most always a victim themselves. Even with that knowledge, gained through working with organizations during my recovery, the topic of forgiveness was not an easy one for me to deal with. In fact, I made a conscious choice to NOT forgive the man. Those in my close group encouraged me to just say it and be done with it. Which I did say, at one point, begrudgingly and in such a way that it caused a small rift in our relationships. Why? Because I was not ready to forgive. I h ad only learned of the abuse a few months before and was still reeling from the reality of what this act had done to my life—and was STILL doing to my life. My perpetrator was dead, and I was still cleaning up his mess. I was angry, hurt, afraid of the future, living alone, and had no visible means of the amount of support I knew I was going to need. I was at the beginning of this journey. No way was I able to even consider forgiving the man, even though I was very familiar with nearly every Bible verse concerning forgiveness. Looking back, I realize now that it was all that scripture that helped me know in the present moment that he needed forgiving. Without that, I do not like to think about where I would be.

Forgiveness is an important choice for an abuse survivor. It is true that unforgiveness leads to bitterness. But forgiveness that is not heartfelt and understood breeds more than bitterness. It compounds the victim's sense of helplessness. Choosing to forgive the perpetrator means being ready to let go of being the victim, regardless of what a situation is involving. I did not want to be a victim; I just needed stability in my own identity as a survivor before I could let the victim in me go away.

I remember the night that all this came out of me. I still wanted someone to come in and rescue me, to come in and console me, or to validate me and me only. I wanted someone to make the bad man go away. Asking me to forgive the man before I had the chance to experience that rescue was wrong, and it's a lesson that I will never forget. As I work with other survivors, I understand more because of that one night how very important it is to give the victim a chance to experience every part of their recovery—and that every part of recovery is necessary, no matter how old a victim is when they disclose.

I truly forgave the man in 2011, during a ministry session for women who were leaving the sex trade industry. I was there ministering with a group of people. A male minister stood before us all and began to talk about forgiveness. It was a divine appointment for me. I was more than ready, well over two years into my recovery, to forgive the man. I just had not thought of doing it.

I had come to understand that his life was much worse than mine. He never got free that I am aware of and died at the age of 51. I knew from others that his family had been riddled with issues that indicated that he had also been sexually abused. I was at a place where I was content with who God was showing me that I was in spite of what had happened to me and how He was using those things in my life to reach out to others. I was reminded that day that, at this point, not forgiving the man would begin to affect my relationship with the Lord.

The male minister stood up and asked the women in the room to allow him to stand in proxy for the men in their lives that had hurt them. I began to weep. My perpetrator wore glasses. This man had on glasses. My perpetrator was a teacher. This man was a spiritual teacher. The women in the room had suffered much more in their lives than I had in mine, but I knew what I had suffered in deciding to forgive. I decided to go to the front, told the women why I had not forgiven the man as of yet, and told them I was now ready to do so.

The male minister, tearfully, took my hands and looked into my face. In his gentle way, he voiced words that I could only imagine the man saying. I closed my eyes and pictured my perpetrator. He told me that he was sorry and that even though bad things might have happened to him, that was no excuse for what he did to me. He apologized for giving me years of heartache. He said that if he could, he would go back in time and change that moment. He asked me for my forgiveness for stealing my innocence. And, I gave it to him. Then, I fell into my Lord's arms again.

I know now that it was one of the hardest things that I will ever have to do in all of my life. But, it was the one moment that I know was made in time just for me. It came through God's leading and His timing, and I meant it with all of my heart. It was more than words out of my mouth; it was an act from the bottom of my heart. And, I became truly free. My favorite rescue fantasy became a reality in the arms of Jesus.

So what did I do with all those other fantasies from the past or present? I learned to separate the fantasies from the heart-felt dreams that I have for my own life. That required a lot of self-research. In order to determine what was real and fantasy, I had to get to know myself—and that meant learning who I was when I was little. I do not remember much from my childhood, typical of most abused children. What I did remember, I used as little clues. I found some really good books and information that helped me self-examine and re-discover what my dreams were as a little child. They never went away; they just got buried under all the bad stuff.

Once discovered, I began to learn how who I grew into colored those dreams in the present. I believe without reservation that every moment of my life, good or bad, is to be used by the Lord for His purposes. So, that means that I had to come to accept myself the way I am and begin walking life from this point on as the person I am, which required me to accept and deal with my past.

One important part was my letting go of trying to be someone that I am not. If I believed that God designed me, then that meant that I had to stop trying to change that design. I am fearfully and wonderfully made, just like everyone else. But, we are all unique in what we are called to do in our lives. Even if that does not look like everyone else, then I was going to need to learn to trust God to be in complete control of my destiny.

This revelation impacts every aspect of life: family, friendships, job situation, ministry, and even romance. Putting it into practice is a daily job. There have been so many times when I wanted to just take control back and do what felt good or what I thought I was best. To be honest, there have been a few times when I did just that. God did not stop me, and I learned the hard way that His way is truly the better way.

What that means is that I have had to put down my own desires for my own life. At the very beginning of recovery, I lived life as if it were all on hold. In my broken mind at the beginning, I thought that I would complete some required amount of time in a "spiritual rehab" and then, magically, my "life" would begin. It only took about a year for me to realize that I was doing something wrong.

When things were not working out, I could see myself as a petulant child, pitching a fit when my own plans did not come out the way I requested. Looking at that one day, I realized that I needed to "grow up." I had to ask for help with this exercise because I had never fully trusted God with my heart or my life, even though I had professed it many times.

This is when I began journaling as mentioned earlier. It grew from a few sentences to pages per entry. As my entries grew, so did my ability to trust God with every part of me. When I look back at some of my heart-felt cries before God, I see now how God answered every cry. These journals are a picture of His faithfulness and unconditional love for ME, because the journals were between Him and myself—not someone else who I was reading about in a book. It is somewhat embarrassing to know that I felt the way I did, but I understand it now. Through that exercise, I also learned to have compassion for myself in a way that nothing else could have taught me. Even though I wrote them, the person reading them is not the same simply because I was changed through the experience of writing of them. Their dual healing purpose was in the present writing and in the future reading.

One of my favorite stories about my journaling time is the time the Lord had me make a list of what I wanted in a man. It seemed like I was supposed to do it, but I told the

Lord, "No, I do not want to because You are just going to show me that I do not need a man." I was only in the first few months of recovery and was petrified that God would make me be alone the rest of my life. At that time, I saw God as a somewhat harsh disciplinarian. His assumed denial of a husband for me was seen as a punishment for my earlier "sins" in life—"You have already had all the men you are going to have, Iris, and now it is My turn. You are mine until the end of time." This was the imagined conversation that I had with the Lord. I knew Him well enough to know that He expected me to at least be willing to be alone if He wanted me to be that way. I just could not make that commitment at that time.

One night, I went to a movie with a friend. In the movie, one of the women was going through a marriage separation. She had been married since she was a young teenager. Her life had become covered up with taking care of a family, a husband, and a home. She had lost herself somewhere along the way. She started filling up a bulletin board with things that she liked and wanted to do. Through it, she rediscovered her life. I left the theatre that night with the full understanding of why I needed to make this list that I had been so opposed to making earlier.

The truth is that I did not have any idea of what I desired in a man. Most of the men in my life, though decent, had so many issues. Those were not what I desired anymore in my life. There was one man that the Lord allowed me to use as a springboard, if you will, for what I really wanted in a man at this new juncture in my life. And, so the list began. I had only met the man once or twice, so I did not know him very well. After 5 or 6 qualities, though, a funny thing happened. I began writing like a fiend. Four pages of "requirements" poured out of me from nowhere. After reading over the list many times, I became discouraged because I knew that no man could ever live up to such a list. I seriously questioned the Lord about this exercise.

About a year later, during one of my journal re-reads, I found this list. I stared at it for a little while. I ask the Lord, why on earth did you have me do this? I glanced over at my bedside table and saw a red pen. Immediately, I knew that I was to start checking off the list. By the time I was through, I realized that the Lord had met every requirement on that list, Himself. He was right; I did not "need" a man. That night, I told the Lord that while I might not NEED a man, I still wanted one in my life. I remember that so clearly. His presence that night was like that of a Father. I could almost feel His arms around me. He whispered in my ear that the list was not about the man—it was about me. I knew what He meant. Without my knowing myself, I could never discern what God's best for me was—whether in a man or anything else—because I first needed to know my own self, inside and out.

Another challenge for me has been not allowing my life to become filled with too much isolation. Living away from friends and family, I struggle with engaging where I am sometimes. I am still working on that. For the first time in 3 years, I am holding a job that puts me in contact with dozens of people on a daily basis. For the first time that I can remember, I am not running away from something in my mind while I am working. Work is not an escape; it is a place where all of the gifts and talents that I have are able to function the way He designed them to work and flow. I look for work to fit who I am instead of trying to conform myself to the parameters of a job. I understand now that a vocation is an expression of the person within. I no longer identify myself with what position I may hold, but allow God to move me as He will to those positions that will best suit who I am and further His Kingdom purposes. I came to understand that every step in my present is planned by Him for a larger purpose that I cannot see. For me, that meant letting go of a conceived notion that I was worthless without a long-term single employment position. This was a key factor in my living without guilt or self-condemnation in my present. I also believe that it is an important key to my unknown and developing future.

As circumstances have played out, I have discovered things about myself that led me to start a business that is suited specifically to who I have grown into. The funny thing is that it is exactly the opposite of who I was trying to be all of my life. And, I am much happier than I ever thought I would ever be. All it took was for me to be willing to let Him work out of me what I did not even know was there. All it took was for me to allow Him to heal me.

This whole healing of self was for myself—not for someone else as I thought at the beginning of my journey into recovery. Learning how to live in the present and getting to know my true self were parts of the necessary healing so that I could be who I have always been called to be. Because of the time spent working on myself, I am happy in my present—for the first time in my entire life.

That, dear Reader, is the reality of my Present.

CHAPTER 5

This last chapter has been the most difficult to write. When we come to the end of a story or book, we expect to have all the loose ends wrapped up into a nice, neat, tidy little package. We want to see the hero with the girl, the kid with a family, the animals making their way home again. We want assurances and guarantees that life will have a happy ending. It is no different for someone who may be writing a story like this.

The beginning of my story started with a death, which is seemingly an end. I think that is fitting that my story ends with an out of character ending—the birth of a future.

The end of my story is that I do not know the end of my story. The end of my story is that every day is a beginning. The end of my story is that I am living a life that would not be possible without the healing power of Jesus and His love for me. It is His love alone that has brought me into the wholeness of who I am now and was always meant to be. I am not late for the things that are happening in my life. Nothing is off-schedule because of what is in my past. The things from my past, my experiences, His revelation, and His healing have made me ready to receive what He still has for me to do in this life.

Sometimes, you can catch a glimpse of who you are and what you are meant to do in life. Those are the snapshots that keep you moving along in the journey. Getting rid of all that mental baggage enables me to believe in His power to have created that person within me. It is not a pride thing to believe that you are better than you think you are—it is a God thing because it takes His healing power to enable you to do something that you cannot do alone sometimes. Every day that I am free to live, dream, and become that person is another opportunity for me to thank Him and live to do the work that He has for me to do—whatever it is.

I believe in that dream not because I desire what comes with the dream. I believe in that dream because of the Giver of the dream and His purposes for that dream. This journey is not about me; it is about the one true God and His great love for the world and for every person in it. If telling the story of what He did for me in my life helps just one person, then it will all have been worth it.

What is my Future? You cannot see me smiling, but I am. I do not know the answer to that question. But, I do not need to know. I am clinging to the One who does and enjoying the journey of a lifetime while He reveals it to me one day at a time. If it is anything like the past, it promises to be better than any eye could behold, any ear could hear, or anyone could ever imagine.

WORKBOOK

FEELINGS

Use these words ALONE to describe how you feel about a situation instead of explaining the situation away in your mind. Speak them out loud in reference to the situation.

For example, someone tells you that they will make dinner for you that night. You anticipate it, wait to eat whatever they will cook, and you get home and you are allergic to whatever they cooked. Instead of saying, "Well they didn't know", etc say something like this:

"I'm really glad you cooked and appreciate the thought, but I can't eat it. I'm mad that I didn't tell you because I'm starving.

It feels like I've hurt you but I'm sorry, I can't eat it—now let's eat a sandwich and talk about what we are going to do tomorrow!"

In using these words, you begin to:
◆ *own all your feelings* which shows self-care
◆ *become aware* of the other person
◆ *resolve the situation* without an incident

Here are the words:

 **ANGRY/MAD**

 **SAD**

 **HURT**

 **AFRAID/SCARED**

 **LONELY**

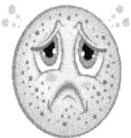 **ASHAMED**

 **HAPPY/GLAD**

MY ART PAGES

Art can be very useful in becoming aware of yourself and feelings that are trying to come out as you begin recovery.

It is also a good way to let go of some things that keep coming up in your mind that are hard to put words to.

If you find yourself thinking about a certain situation more than a couple of times:

◆ pick up the pencils
◆ begin to draw what you are seeing (no one will see it but you)
◆ come back and put the words that you feel around the pictures

These instructions are coming from personal experience and should be reviewed with your doctor. You may want them to review your drawings as well.

AFFIRMATIONS

Abuse of any kind injures more than just a person's self-esteem. In some ways, the brain itself suffers as well. While attending a short mind/body health class after the diagnosis of cancer, I learned that when the body suffers a trauma, the mind suffers as well. We were taught that short, repetitive tasks were healing to the brain and emotions. I saw this principle work many times. Simple tasks, such as washing dishes or ironing clothes, were times that I could allow my brain to focus on the task at hand to the point where all other thoughts left my brain except for what my hands were doing.

Using the same principle was a little more challenging when working with my self-esteem. Nevertheless, it WAS still the same principle. I often hear the term "meditation" while in recovery. No one ever really explained how to do it, though. I conjured up images of sitting cross-legged on the floor, incense burning in the background—not images that I was really comfortable with, however. Another term kept coming up: "personal affirmations." Again, I had no clue what all that meant; or more than that, I had no idea how to "do" any of that.

I learned that I needed to pour into my self-esteem new material, on a regular basis, very purposefully. Saying something, or reading something one time and wanting to believe it was not enough. So, I researched until I found a website that offered some of the most self-compassionate self-talk that I have yet to come across. The only challenge was that they were not specific enough for me in their crediting the source of their strength.

What follows is my faith-influenced adaptation of a wonderful principle from a secular source. After reading them many times, I realized that over time, the Lord moved me away from these and into His word where I found these again and so much more.

Reading these on a regular basis became my meditation, or as I like to call it, my medication. My brain desperately needed these simple statements on a regular basis.

Read these over yourself on a regular basis. Focus on one or a few at a time.

I am now celebrating life, having fun, and enjoying myself.

I am radiantly good-looking, vibrantly healthy, and joyously alive.

I am a magnificent spiritual being, full of Light and Love.

God wants me to be happy, healthy, loved, and successful.

The Light within me is creating miracles in my life here and now.

Abundance is my natural state of being. I accept it now.

All of my experiences are opportunities to gain more power, clarity, and vision.

I am a radiant expression of Christ within.

I am always at the right place, at the right time, successfully engaged in the right activity.[*]

---

[*]   Copied from and based on Robert Burney's Positive Affirmations, from Robert Burney and Joy to You & Me Enterprises, http://joy2meu.com/PositiveAffirmations.html

PERSONALITY QUIRKS?

The first time I ever realized that my personality had quirks was at a conference in Pensacola, FL, during the late 1990's where *Charisma* magazine writer, Steve Beard, was speaking. He explained that the very issue in our life that was causing us the most grief was quite possibly the very GIFT that God had placed within us that was to be used in a positive way. Did I ever feel a spiritual whiplash of sorts that day! He went on to explain that the enemy, while not all-knowing, could recognize spiritual gifts and would work to try to destroy them—or us with them. That was just the beginning of my education.

Through the years, I played with personality tests and learned more about myself. However, it wasn't until I had laid my soul bare before the Lord, and emptied myself of every thing that had been in me since my earliest childhood memories, did I even begin to understand a few keyw things.

First, God made me. He has always known who I would become, with my childhood and issues factored in.

Second, He loves me IN SPITE of that.

Third, for me to put myself down for ANY reason is to speak against God's creation.

Fourth, I must recognize, accept, forgive, and be willing to help restore any part of myself that is in me.

Until I have done those 4 things, any work I do on myself is basically going nowhere. Those 4 things put gas in my tank, if you will, for my recovery.

How did I do this? Well, first of all, after I realized that there was a wounded part of me holding on, I called out to the Lord to show me what to do. He, through a dear friend, helped me understand how to speak to that part of myself. I learned that the hurting part of me was the 3 year old who had been violated. By writing the little girl in me a letter, I acknowledged her for the first time in my life as a vital part of who I am rather than berating her for existing still. That part of my mind was protecting me from a horrible secret. It was, however, because of her bravery to hold that secret that I managed to grow up. Now, it was time for her to go back to being a child and let the grown up Iris have that memory so that we could both heal. (See Appendix A, page 75, for Letter to Little Iris.)

The result of that "conversation" was the process that this workbook attempts to assist with.

Through the last couple of years, I have take several personality tests and spiritual giftings tests to help me uncover the very deep roots of my personality. In addition, I asked several trusting individuals to wrote a few words about how they viewed me—negative as well as positive. I called it "Myself Through the Eyes of Others."

You see, it is important to accept that a portion of who we are RIGHT NOW is exactly who we are supposed to be. The entire slate of one's life cannot be wiped clean. All experiences, relationships, and decisions that we have and have made go into making us we who are. By being strong enough to ask those who know love us to give us input, we are taking a huge step in learning to trust others and ourselves. We are taking an inventory of ourselves that will provide us with an overview of who we are, the good and the bad. Together, with the Lord and an accountability partner, we can begin to allow God to restore us, resurrect our dreams, rejuvenate the pure heart that He placed within us for His purposes and so that we may fulfill the plans that He has for our individual lives.

Please see the Resource List for a few websites to assist you in integrating all of your experiences into the person that He desires you to be.

THINGS I LIKE...

About God: _____

_____

_____

_____

_____

_____

To see in people: _____

_____

_____

_____

_____

_____

About my family: _____

_____

_____

_____

_____

About my friends: _____

_____

_____

_____

_____

About myself: _____
_____
_____
_____
_____

Go back and circle in red the things that make you decide if you will "choose" to stay connected to someone, either in the moment or in the relationship.

THINGS I DON'T LIKE...

About God: _____

_____

_____

_____

_____

To see in people: _____

_____

_____

_____

_____

About my family: _____

_____

_____

_____

_____

About my friends: _____

_____

_____

_____

_____

About myself: _____

_____

_____

_____

_____

Go back and circle in blue the things that make you decide if you will "choose" to NOT stay connected to someone,
either in a given moment or in the relationship.

WHEN I GROW UP, I WANT TO BE...

What we played the most as children is usually indicative of the gifts and talents that God placed within us. Usually a pattern emerges when recalled and written down. In doing this exercise, a fog can be lifted in the area of seeing ourselves as He created us.

TOYS I LIKE/LIKED TO PLAY WITH: (action figures, dolls, building blocks, crayons)

_____

_____

_____

GAMES I LIKE/LIKED TO PLAY WITH: (video, sports, cards, board games)

_____

_____

_____

ACTIVITIES I LIKE/LIKED TO PARTICIPATE IN: (block parties, sports, crafts, reading, church, hiking)

_____

_____

_____

PLACES I HAVE VISITED THAT I REMEMBER CLEARLY: (relatives, amusement parks, cities)

_____

_____

_____

YOUR CALLING

Only God knows your true calling, but He gives us clues because He gives us free choice in accepting our calling. Sometimes, the enemy clouds our view of our true calling to keep us from reaching our destiny. With His guidance, He lifts the fog put in us by the enemy and allows us to see ourselves as He has always seen us—His children with a specific purpose, a specific job that only you were created to fill.

A song that has ministered to me is: *Here I Am* by Downhere by Jason Germain, Marc Martel (2009)

http://www.youtube.com/watch?v=Thn4fgLvOfo
http://www.downhere.com/

What verses do you feel God has given you
that you have remembered?

What are some verses that you marked in your Bible
and a couple of words regarding their point:

Who are some of your favorite Bible heroes and why?

What stories do you remember MOST from the Bible,
without thinking too hard?

What is the one thing you would HATE
for your calling to be?

What part of ministry do you enjoy the most?

What part of God's nature do you see
in the thing that you enjoy the most?

In your opinion, what invitation from Him
would be the best invitation from Him be to do with your
life?

Who is already doing what you want God
to have in store for you?

DAILY SCHEDULE

Iris tips for filling in your schedule

◆ Write down the most basic things (wake, dress, shower)
◆ Leave time for computer, phone, work, meals
◆ Schedule your sleeping time
◆ Schedule your fun time (in name only)
◆ For devotional & homework time, write down 3 or less sources you will use and change schedule when those are completed.
◆ Use blocks of time to offer more freedom within hours (i.e. 8a-1p: Work)
◆ Build the schedule to mirror your goal as much as possible not to reflect 100% the way things are now.

5:00am_____

6:00am_____

7:00am_____

8:00am_____

9:00am_____

10:00am_____

11:00am_____

12:00pm_____

1:00pm_____

2:00pm_____

3:00pm_____

4:00pm_____

5:00pm_____

6:00pm_____

7:00pm_____

8:00pm_____

9:00pm_____

10:00pm_____

11:00pm_____

12:00am_____

I AM WHAT I EAT...

There are countless sources to discuss the value of eating healthfully. I am in no way a nutritionist. I can, however, attest to the truth that what we eat and drink completely affects all parts of lives: mind, body, and spirit. I can also attest that my mind, body, and spirit influence what I eat.

As I walk through recovery, I can see how my emotions and attitude affect my choices. When I feel really good about myself, I want to make good choices. When I am striving to maintain emotional balance, my choices are careless.

As far back as I can remember, I have eaten out nearly every day. Eating out is easier than cooking for two. Some might say I am over-analyzing in this next statement, but by following this routine from early childhood, I learned to ignore nurturing myself. Remember, abused children are taught through another's actions that they are worthless. So, why would someone who thinks they are worthless take the time to THINK or CARE about what food they put into their bodies? This habit has continued most of my life, to the point of feeding my body many dangerous chemicals over my lifetime.

During 2000 and 2001, after the cancer diagnosis, I learned just how dangerous my eating habits were. I asked for help at my doctor's office and met with a nutritionist. She taught me "how to shop safely" and explained to me the consequences of unchanged choices. Processed foods contain chemicals and materials that we were never meant to digest. Couple that with hereditary issues and physical conditions, a recipe for potential disaster abounds.

Taken from another source,* here, in a nutshell are the foundational needs that we need:

1. Water - pure and clean (not chlorinated)
2. Minerals and vitamins from whole foods
3. Essential fatty acids from Omega 3 and 6 oils
4. Enzymes from living plants
5. Friendly bacteria (probiotics)
6. Plant based proteins

I am not a "meat hater" or a vegetarian. I like meat. However, my body requires little meat to maintain health. Too much meat makes me feel bad, physically and mentally. I am sure that all the hormones that go into our meat supply have something to do with that also, but I will leave that topic for another day!

Another substance that was removed was caffeine. After one too many rounds with rebound headaches, I realized one day that caffeine is a drug. Doctors and drug manufacturers use caffeine as a drug—it IS a drug. Why was I choosing to put a DRUG into my body? After deciding to eliminate this addictive chemical from my diet, my choices have been limited, severely at times, due to this decision. However, I cannot tell you how this one decision in 2009 changed my life for the better. I can only say that every person needs to discover for themselves what is best for them.

----

   *   Christine Pedersen — Nutritional Consultant / Blood Analyst "Food Therapy for Depression,"
http://www.jaredstory.com/depression_food_therapy.html

The nutritionist suggested an easy formula for success: shop the outside walls of the grocery store. Think about it. What is on the walls in most stores? Produce, meat, dairy, and bread. More correctly, whole foods. In other words, things that don't come in a box or a can. Boxes and cans mean processing. Processing means chemicals. Chemicals wreak havoc in our bodies and on our organs. While complete eradication of processed foods may not be feasible, curbing consumption of such things is a reasonable goal. This was the beginning for me: shop the outside walls and stay out of the middle of the store whenever possible.

Even though prices are a concern—face it, manufacturers don't make it easy to eat healthy—eating healthy is possible. We owe it to ourselves to put into our bodies what we need to feel physically good so that we can maintain a healthy mental state. Food is not our source for happiness, but what we feed ourselves is the gas that fills our body's tank as we fill our spiritual tank with the love of the Lord and His goodness. You can't run well on one without the other. They go hand in hand.

I never saw with complete understanding how my emotions were driving my eating. I love to eat; I love to cook for other people; and, quite honestly, cooking and preparing food is one of my gifts. I see that now. I now see food as gas. Good gas means great gas mileage—physically and mentally. Proper amounts are another part of that. Moderation is the key to everything in life, it seems. I understand now why my need for feeling in control was driving even my eating habits.

I still see this at various times in my life when I open my cabinet doors. Right now, I have numerous items in my cabinet that I purchased at emotional times. I ate a portion during my emotional episode and never finished the box. My root choices have changed, so my "right mind" won't let me eat the food during "normal times." I keep them there to remind myself of my past choices and to help me discipline myself. I am not always successful; but, I am far better than I used to be about food in times of emotional upset.

One a final note, over the last couple of years, I have really become aware of how easy it is to WANT to eat the right things since I have been dealing with the effects of abuse. Again, that's not to say that some of my habits aren't still there. It's just getting a lot easier to discipline myself now that the emotional roots have been and are being dealt with. Once something is brought into the light, darkness loses its hold—in so many areas.

JOURNAL PAGES

_____

_____

_____

_____

_____

_____

_____

_____

_____

_____

_____

_____

_____

_____

_____

_____

_____

_____

_____

_____

_____

_____

_____

_____

_____

_____

_____

_____

_____

_____

_____

LITERARY RESOURCES

Below is a partial list of many books and websites that I have been led to at various times during this journey. I read one book as far back as the late 1990's; another one was completed just before this book was published. So, you can see that healing is an on-going journey. The only day we truly be finished healing is the day we are ushered into His presence for the rest of eternity.

Please understand, these publications and websites in no way took the place of the healing love, mercy, and grace of Jesus in my life. It is with full confidence and trust in Him alone that I know He gave me the courage to read and learn about my issues. Finding each of these was also subject to His special timing—*Kairos* Time— never a minute late or second early. Some of these materials are secular; a lot of them are faith-based; all of them healed me to some degree. To Him be all the glory for each of them.

The most important thing to remember is that no matter where we are, where we go, or where we end up, the Lord Himself is our guide, our companion, our comfort, and our shield. Always has; always will be. Please don't ever forget that. I hope that you, or anyone that you know, will find the courage to begin, continue, or complete the journey of healing from childhood sexual abuse.

BEAUTY

Hilson, Cynthia. *Esther's Days of Purification*. Precious Oils Up On the Hill. 2010. ISBN:978-0982687802. Scriptural study of apothecary and its merits.

Rubin, Elycia and Rita Mauceri. *Frumpy to Foxy in 15 Minutes Flat.* Fair Winds Press. 2005. ISBN:978-1592331109 . Style advice for every woman.

Terri, Joy. *The Make-up Book: Every Woman's Guide to the Art of Applying Make-up.* New Holland. 2002. ISBN:978-1859740996.

DEVOTIONALS

Adams, Michelle Medlock. *Secrets of Beauty.* Barbour Publications. 2005. ISBN:978-1593109110. A 60-day devotional for the inner you.

Beattie, Melody. *The Language of Letting Go.* Mjf Books. 1998. ISBN:978-1567312386. A recovery devotional.

Donihue, Anita Corrine. *When God Calls Me Blessed:Devotional Thoughts for Women from the Beautitudes.* Barbour Publishing. 2002. ISBN:978-1586605728.

The Life Recovery Bible. Tyndale House Publishing. 1992. ISBN:978-0842320832. The Living Bible with 12-Step devotionals and life application lessons.

LOVE, MARRIAGE, AND INTIMACY

Chapman, Gary. *The Five Love Languages for Singles.* Northfield Publishing. 2004. ISBN:978-1881273981. How different personalities express love in different ways.

Chitwood, Melanie. *What a Husband Needs from His Wife: Physically*Emotionally*Spiritually.* Harvest House Publishers. 2006. ISBN:978-0736918305.

Evans, Jimmy. *Our Secret Paradise*. Regal Books. 2006. ISBN:978-0830739042. Seven secrets for building a secure and satisfying marriage.

Gardner, Tim Alan. *Sacred Sex: A Spiritual Celebration of Oneness in Marriage*. WaterBrook Press. 2002. ISBN:9781578564613.

Hammond, Michelle McKinney and Joel A. Brooks Jr. *What Women Don't Know (And Men Don't Tell You) The Unspoken Rules of Finding Lasting Love*. WaterBrook Press. 2009. ISBN:978-0307458506.

Hammond, Michelle McKinney. *What To Do Until Love Finds You: The Bestselling Guide to Preparing Yourself for Your Perfect Mate*. Harvest House Publishers. 2006. ISBN:978-0736917186.

Jaynes, Sharon. *Becoming the Woman of His Dreams: Seven Qualities Every Man Longs For*. Harvest House Publishers. 2005. ISBN:978-0736913515.

Ludy, Eric and Leslie. *When God Writes your Love Story: The Ultimate Approach to Guy/Girl Relationships*. Multnomah Books. 2004. ISBN:978-1590523520.

DiMarco, Hayley and Michael. *The Art of the First Date: Because Dating's Not A Science – It's An Art*. Revell Books. 2006. ISBN: 978-0800731489.

DiMarco, Hayley and Michael. *The Art of Rejection: Because Dating's Not A Science – It's An Art*. Revelle Books. 2006. ISBN:978-0800731465.

Munro, Myles. *Waiting and Dating: A Sensible Guide to a Fulfilling Love Relationship*. Destiny Image. 2005. ISBN:978-0768421576.

Prince, Derek with Ruth Prince. *God Is A Match-Maker*. Chosen A Division of Baker Book House. 1986. ISBN:978-0800790585.

Scanlon, Bethany K. *Where's My Mate?*. Xulon Press. 2006. ISBN:978-1597819428.

Sumrall, Lester. *60 Things God Said About Sex*. Whitaker House. 2002. ISBN:978-0883687703. God made us to be sexual creatures and we ought to understand the pattern He intended for us to follow in our sexual relationships.

Wilkerson, David. *Have You Felt Like Giving Up Lately?* Revell Books. 1982. ISBN:978-0800784812.

MENTAL HEALTH

Bates, Tony. *Understanding and Overcoming Depression: A Common Sense Approach*. Crossing Press. 2000. ISBN:978-1580910316.

Simon, David MD and Deepak Chopra, MD. *Freedom from Addiction*: *The Chopra Center Method for Overcoming Destructive Habits*. HCI. 2007. ISBN:978-0757305788.

Stroshahl, Kirk PhD and Patricia Robinson, PhD. *The Mindfulness and Acceptance Workbook for Depression:Using Acceptance and Commitment Therapy to Move Through Depression and Create a Life Worth Living*. New Harbinger Publications. 2008. ISBN:978-1572245488.

PHYSICAL HEALTH

Colbert, Don MD. *The Bible Cure for Cancer: Ancient Truths, Natural Remedies and the Latest Findings for Your Health Today.* Siloam. 1999. ISBN:978-0884196259.

D'Adamo, Peter J. and Catherine Whitney. *Eat Right 4 Your Type.* Century. 1998. ISBN:978-0712677165. The Individualized diet solution to staying healthy, living longer and achieving your ideal weight.

Wright, Henry W. *A More Excellent Way: Be in Health.* Pleasant Valley. 2003. ISBN:978-0967805929.

SEXUAL ABUSE

Bass, Ellen and Laura Davis. *Beginning to Heal: A First Book for Men and Women Who Were Sexually Abused as Children.* HarperCollins Publishers. 2003. ISBN:978-0060564698.

Bass, Ellen and Laura Davis. *The Courage to Heal: A Guide for Women Survivors of Child Sexual Abuse: 20th Anniversary Edition.* HarperCollins Publishers. 2008. ISBN:978-0061284335.

Fredrickson, Renee PhD. *Repressed Memories: A Journey to Recovery from Sexual Abuse.* Touchstone. 1992. ISBN:978-0671767167.

Murphy, Cecil. *When a Man You Loved Was Abused: A Woman's Guide to Helping Him Overcome Childhood Sexual Molestation.* Kregel Publications. 2010. ISBN:978-082543353.

Scales, Tom. *Terrible Things Happened to Me: A True Story of Violence and Victory.* Self-Published. 2011. ISBN:978-1604143973.

Tuggle, Brad and Cheryl. *A Healing Marriage: Biblical Help for Overcoming Childhood Sexual Abuse.* NavPress. 2004. ISBN:978-1576836029.

Williams, Angela. *From Sapphires to Sorrows: Breaking the Silence of Child Sexual Abuse.* Paracomm Media Group. 2008. ISBN:978-0976087601.

Spiritual

Copeland, Gloria. *God's Master Plan for Your Life: Ten Keys to Fulfilling Your Destiny.* Berkley Trade. 2009. ISBN:978-0425228593.

Earley, Dave. *21 Reasons Bad Things Happen to Good People.* Barbour Publishing. 2008. ISBN:978-1602602199. If God is good, why does He allow suffering?

Evans, Tony. *Let It Go! Breaking Free from Fear and Anxiety.* Moody Publishers. 2005. ISBN:978-0802443786.

Kendall, R.T. *God Meant It for Good: A Fresh Look at the Life of Joseph.* MorningStar Publications. 2003. ISBN:978-1878327307.

Manning, Brennan. *Ruthless Trust: The Ragamuffin's Path to God.* HarperCollins. 2002. ISBN:978-0062517760.

Neufeld, Jody. *Grief: Finding the Candle of Light.* Energion Publications. 2007. ISBN:978-1893729506.

Prince, Derek. *Entering the Presence of God.* Whitaker House. 2007. ISBN:978-0883687192.

Prince, Derek. *God's Remedy for Rejection.* Whitaker House. 2002. ISBN:978-0883688649.

Towns, Elmer L. *Fasting for Spiritual Breakthrough: A Guide to Nine Biblical Fasts.* Regal. 1996. ISBN:978-0830718399.

Wright, Henry W. *Insights Into: Addictions.* Be in Health. 2007. ISBN:978-1934680124.

WOMEN'S ISSUES

Ethridge, Shannon. *Every Woman's Battle: Discovering God's Plan for Sexual and Emotional Fulfillment.* WaterBrook. 2003. ISBN:978-1578566853.

George, Elizabeth. *Life Management for Busy Women: Living Out God's Plan with Passion and Purpose.* Harvest House Publishers. 2002. ISBN:978-0736901918.

Heald. Cynthia. *A Woman's Journey to the Heart of God.* Thomas Nelson Publishers. 1997. ISBN:978-0785272397.

Heald, Cynthia. *A Journal for the Journey.* Thomas Nelson Publishers. 1997. ISBN:978-0785271260.

Jakes, Serita Ann. *The Princess Within: Restoring the Soul of a Woman.* Bethany House. 2002. ISBN:978-0764227479.

Jaynes, Sharon. *"I'm Not Good Enough" and Other Lies Women Tell Themselves.* Harvest House Publishers. 2009. ISBN:978-0736918701.

Kendall, Jackie and Debby Jones. *Lady In Waiting: Becoming God's Best While Waiting for Mr. Right.* Destiny Image. 2005. ISBN:978-0768423105.

McMenamin, Cindi. *When A Woman Discovers Her Dream: Finding God's Purpose for Your Life.* Harvest House Publishers. 2005. ISBN:978-0736914123.

Partow. Donna. *Becoming the Woman God Wants Me to Be: A 90-Day Guide to Living the Proverbs 31 Life.* Revell. 2008. ISBN:978-0800730727.

Thomas, Angela. *Do You Think I'm Beautiful.* Thomas Nelson. 2005. ISBN:978-0785273776. The question every woman asks.

Web Resources

We are certainly blessed in these times to have so much information at our fingertips. It would be careless to provide these sites and articles without stating that not every word available at our fingertips is 100% ordained by the Lord. Please be mindful of the time that is devoted to this portion of healing. Something that is free and readily available can easily take a place in life that it was not meant to have. Information is meant to complement other recovery tools, not to become the only one.

When researching, it is usually best to stick to reputable sites that have nothing to gain by your reading their information. Their only "payment" should be the furthering of your knowledge. That is not to say that there may not be times that payment for a service might not be required, such as a personal consultation on a beauty site, for example. Also, you may find some sites set up by individuals that really strike a chord in you for some reason. Trust the Holy Spirit in you, and possibly them, to have you there for a reason that is particular to you and your recovery. Know also that the Lord is bigger than any article that you may find that might NOT have been meant for good. He can use whatever He desires, whenever He needs to, and however He deems fit for the individual that He is working with—mainly you, the reader, at this point. And He is able to undo any wrong information that you might, and probably will, come across in your recovery journey. Trust Him to take care of you. What worked for one person, may not work for the next person. That is the beauty of our God; He tailors healing to the person seeking Him for their healing.

[Note: The articles notated here were accessed on July 17, 2012.]

BEAUTY

Carol Thompson Beauty Secrets. http://www.carolthompsonbeautysecrets.com/

Look Fabulous. http://www.look-fabulous.com/

Makeup Geek. http://www.makeupgeek.com/

TEB Associates International. "Determining Your Tonal Seasons," http://trepanrr.tripod.com/color_analysis_test.htm#your_personal_makeup_palette

LOVE, MARRIAGE, AND INTIMACY

Aurora Health Care. "Overcoming Fear of Intimacy," http://www.aurorahealthcare.org/yourhealth/healthgate/getcontent.asp?URLhealthgate=%2214278.html%22

SixWise:Epiphanies for Your Empowerment. "Over-Analyzing Versus Fully Inhabiting Your Intimate Relationship," http://www.sixwise.com/newsletters/06/04/19/over-analyzing-versus-fully-inhabiting-your-intimate-relationship.htm

Suite101. "Overcoming Fear of Intimacy for People in Love," http://suite101.com/article/overcoming-fear-of-intimacy-a10261

MENTAL HEALTH

Joy 2 ME U:Abundant Spritualiy + Codependency Recovery + Inner Child Healing + Love = Joy2MEU. "Internal
Boundaries: The Key to Balance,"
   http://joy2meu.com/internal_boundaries.html

_____. "More on Positive Affirmations: Taking More Lov-
ing Action for Our Self,"
   http://joy2meu.com/PositiveAffirmations.htm

Lahey Clinic: A Teaching Hospital of Tufts University
School of Medicine. "Post-Traumatic Stress Disorder," http://
health.nytimes.com/health/guides/disease/hypothalam-
ic-dysfunction/overview.html

Livestrong: The Limitless Potential of You. "Model of
Self-Esteem,"
   http://www.livestrong.com/article/14676-mod-
el-of-self-esteem/

Sexual Control: Successful Sex Addiction Counseling
Since 1983. http://www.sexualcontrol.com/index.php

PHYSICAL HEALTH

The New York Times: Health. " Hypothalamic Dysfunction,"
   http://health.nytimes.com/health/guides/disease/hy-
pothalamic-dysfunction/overview.html

Sexual Abuse

American Academy of Experts in Traumatic Stress. "Sexual Abuse: Surviving the Pain,"
  http://www.aaets.org/article31.htm

American Psychological Association. "Understanding Child Sexual Abuse: Education, Prevention, and Recovery,"
http://www.apa.org/pubs/info/brochures/sex-abuse.aspx#

Boulware, Carol MFT, Ph.D. "Adult Survivors of Childhood Sexual Abuse,"
  http://www.psychotherapist.net/adultsurvivors.html

DC Rape Crisis Center: Support & Counseling. "Adult Survivors of Child Sexual Abuse," http://www.dcrcc.org/
support_counseling/adult_survivors_of_child_sexual_abuse/
C121/emotional_effects1/

Munro, Kali Psychotherapist. "Trusting Your Memories of Child Abuse,"
  http://kalimunro.com/wp/articles-info/sexual-emotional-abuse/trusting-your-memories-of-sexual-abuse

Voice Today. "Breaking the Cycle of Child Sexual Abuse,"
http://www.voicetoday.org/

Spiritual

Beattie, Melody. "Living in the Mystery," http://melody-beattie.com/

Navarre Beach Side Church: The Church Without Walls. "Deliverance,"
  http://www.beachsidechurch.com/jesus/heals.html

Appendix A

Dear Little Iris,

I have heard so much about you through pictures and stories. I even remember some things about you on my own. I am writing this letter to talk to you, Little Iris. I hope you will listen and know that I love you as you are reading this.

Recently, a part of me grew up—actually, it has been a long time coming; but in doing so, it was brought to my attention that you are still very much in control of my everyday life because you are holding on to some very heavy information regarding our past. Is this true?

Oh sweet little girl, how wonderful you are to have protected me all these years. How brave you have been, little baby. What an awesome little soldier you have been, warring for us all these years. I'm a warrior, too, little girl. Our Heavenly Father taught me how to war. Isn't it funny that the school mascot for all those years was a warrior—I guess that set our tone, huh?

You went through so much. How did you manage? It was because of Him, wasn't it? You knew He was there all along, but in such a special way. He was protecting you when you couldn't protect yourself. Did you know that? He loves us both so much, you the helpless, little child and me, the full-grown woman. We are the same, Little Iris. We always were.

I'm so sorry that you suffered. All those times that you were playing with the dolls and animals, you loved them the way that you desired to be loved. God's love was already in you. You always went for the underdog because inside, you felt and were one too. You were such a good protector all those years, not only to me, but to other children as well. Because of the brokenness in you, you were drawn to other ones who were broken, too. Even as a small child, you were already putting the bad to work for Him; how much I appreciate that about you now, Little Iris. Thank you for feeling His leading and being obedient to Him for us that way. Such a sweet little baby, and so beautiful and full of life. You battled back by never giving up and by protecting me as I was coming out. You even kept on right up until now.

I'm sorry that I didn't know what you were going through. I'm sorry that I did things that dishonored the protection that you were giving us. I'm sorry that I didn't understand all these years that the actions you were doing were your way of crying out about the pain that you suffered. I'm so sorry that I didn't take better care of us through the years, Little Iris. I'm sorry that I did things that put us into jeopardy. I'm sorry that I thought you were a bad person when you were just crying out because of your pain. I pray that He never takes His hand off either of us. We are so special to Him, truly His princess.

You were and are so beautiful. It was that shining quality that was the draw that brought the pain. The darkness hates the light and seeks to destroy it. But that wasn't your fault. And, you battled back from that the best way that you could. The enemy battled by affecting your mind, making you think you were ugly and unworthy of the best that life had to offer. But, our God made war for us by burying those ugly memories far into the recesses of our mind knowing that one day we could be whole because of His love and be ready to rid ourselves of this once and for all. The best that life had to offer is still out there for us; He's been holding it for us. Because of Him you did your job so well that the painful memories are still with you, my little warrior princess.

But, Little Iris, it's time for you to give those awful memories to me now. The armor that I wear is now protecting us both, baby. You are safe now, under the shelter of His wings over us both. No one will ever hurt you again; the pain will not hurt me either because He holds me now, too. You can give that heavy weight back, not to me, but to Jesus—our knight in shining armor. He is going to hold onto that weight now. I can't hold it, but He will let me know what I need to know. You don't have to be afraid of that for me anymore. You don't have to protect us any longer, because He is protecting us both. I want you to let them go. It won't hurt me. And you'll never be hurt again. You are safe with me and under His wings. I know you must be so tired of holding onto such memories. Come to me this morning and let me love on you the way that you deserved to be loved. I accept you; you are such a good girl. There is not one little girl that I know that is better than you have been. I am so proud of you, Little Iris, for being who you have been.

I promise to begin to honor you, little girl. I want you to come back to me. I never really got to know you, baby girl. He wants us to have fun, sweetie. You are so needed in my life. You've been doing such a good job being a grown up, but it's time for you to put down that job that was thrown onto you and go back to being the child that you never had a chance to be. I'm so proud of you, Little Iris. And I love you so much; please come back to me. I need you with me, doing the job that you never really got a chance to do. There is so much that you never got to do. It's our time now. Please don't be afraid. He'll take care of us both.

Come to me in a dream, my sweet baby girl. I want to meet you, face to face. I'll be waiting.

Love,
Big Girl Iris

God's Promise of Marriage

Iris Subel Davis

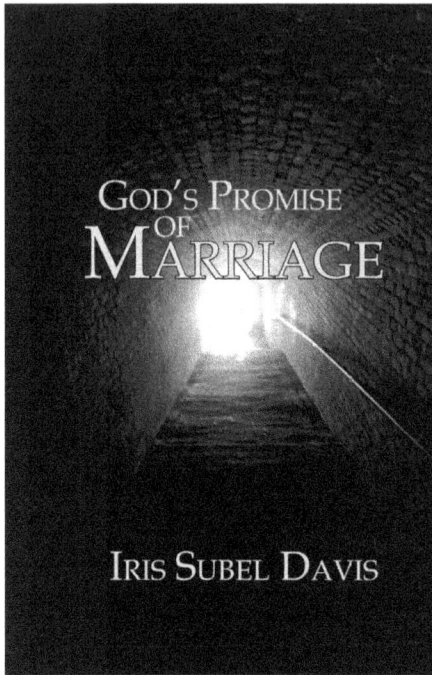

A well-built, young 5'9" man jerks violently forward, waving an accusing finger into the defensive face of a 5'3" woman. Voices raise decibels above yelling. The petite woman steadfastly holds and defends her ground. Words mix together with raging emotions of anger, shame, guilt, fear, frustration, and resolve while an overwhelming cloud of fight-or-flight hangs over the entire confrontation. In the next room, a baby is asleep. Off to the side in another bedroom doorway, a younger woman stands observing the entire situation in shock disguised as calm. Words and actions wash over her as she processes the volatile event. The door jamb becomes more than a support for her body as the weight of her life's choices evolve in an instant. "Lord, how did I get here? Is this what you have for me? Is this what marriage is all about? I promise that if you get him out of here tonight, I will be in church tomorrow. I'll give you my life, for real this time." A single promise became the key to the redemption of more than just one life.

Find out how the power of Jesus Christ transformed the author, her marriage, and the future.

Coming in 2013 from EnerPower Press
EnerPowerPress.com

MORE FROM ENERGION PUBLICATIONS

Personal Study
It's in the Bag	Kimberly Gordon	$5.99
Victim No More!	Shauna Hyde	$12.99
When People Speak for God	Henry Neufeld	$17.99
The Sacred Journey	Chris Surber	$11.99
Gomorrah Was Religious Too	Chris Surber	$9.99
Words of Life, Light, and Love	Betty Rae Nick	$7.99

Christian Living
Be an Encourager	Diane Milnes	$7.99
Grief: Finding the Candle of Light	Jody Neufeld	$8.99
I Want to Pray	Perry M. Dalton	$7.99
Crossing the Street	Robert LaRochelle	$16.99
Daily Devotions of Ordinary People - Extraordinary God	Jody Neufeld	$19.99

Bible Study
Learning and Living Scripture	Lentz/Neufeld	$12.99
From Inspiration to Understanding	Edward W. H. Vick	$24.99
Luke: A Participatory Study Guide	Geoffrey Lentz	$8.99
Philippians: A Participatory Study Guide	Bruce Epperly	$9.99
Ephesians: A Participatory Study Guide	Robert D. Cornwall	$9.99
Hebrews: A Participatory Study Guide	Henry E. Neufeld	$9.99
Revelation: A Participatory Study Guide	Henry E. Neufeld	$9.99

Theology
Ultimate Allegiance	Robert D. Cornwall	$9.99
The Church Under the Cross	William Powell Tuck	$11.99
The Journey to the Undiscovered Country	William Powell Tuck	$9.99

Ministry
Soup Kitchen for the Soul	Renee Crosby	$12.99
Out of This World	Darren McClellan	$24.99

Generous Quantity Discounts Available
Energion Publications — P.O. Box 841
Gonzalez, FL 32560
Website: http://energionpubs.com
Phone: (850) 525-3916

www.ingramcontent.com/pod-product-compliance
Lightning Source LLC
Chambersburg PA
CBHW031604040426
42452CB00006B/406